CATH
TEAC
ON THE
SHOAH

IMPLEMENTING THE HOLY SEE'S
WE REMEMBER

SECRETARIAT FOR ECUMENICAL AND INTERRELIGIOUS AFFAIRS
NATIONAL CONFERENCE OF CATHOLIC BISHOPS

UNITED STATES CATHOLIC CONFERENCE
WASHINGTON, D.C.

At its November 1999 meeting, the Bishops' Committee for Ecumenical and Interreligious Relations discussed and approved the publication of these reflections as a resource for use on all levels of Catholic education. At its September 2000 meeting, the Administrative Committee of the National Conference of Catholic Bishops also discussed and approved it for publication. It has been reviewed by Bishop Tod D. Brown, the chairman of the BCEIA and approved for publication by the undersigned.

Msgr. Dennis M. Schnurr
General Secretary, NCCB/USCC

Cover: Pope John Paul II at Western Wall in Jerusalem, March 26, 2000. Photo by CNS/Reuters.

List of resources based in part on a bibliography compiled by Ned Shulman, © 1990, for *The Holocaust: A Guide for Pennsylvania Teachers*, by Gary M. Grobman. Used with permission from the copyright holder.

First Printing, February 2001

ISBN 1-57455-406-9

Contents

Catholic Teaching on the *Shoah*

Implementing the Holy See's *We Remember*

O n March 23, 2000, at Yad Vashem, Jerusalem—Israel's memorial to the Six Million—His Holiness Pope John Paul II spoke of the need to remember:

In this place of memories, the mind and heart and soul feel an extreme need for silence. Silence in which to remember. Silence in which to try to make some sense of the memories which come flooding back. Silence because there are no words strong enough to deplore the terrible tragedy of the *Shoah* [i.e., the Holocaust]. My own personal memories are of all that happened when the Nazis occupied Poland during the War. I remember my Jewish friends and neighbors, some of whom perished while others survived.

I have come to Yad Vashem to pay homage to the millions of Jewish people who, stripped of everything, especially of their human dignity, were murdered in the Holocaust. More than half a century has passed, but the memories remain.

Here, as at Auschwitz and many other places in Europe, we are overcome by the echo of the heart-rending laments of so many. Men, women and children cry out to us from the depths of the horror they knew. How can we fail to heed their cry? No one can forget or ignore what happened. No one can diminish its scale.

1

We wish to remember. But we wish to remember for a purpose, namely to ensure that never again will evil prevail as it did for the millions of innocent victims of Nazism.

How could man have such utter contempt for man? (nos. 1-2)

A WORD ON THE PRESENT DOCUMENT

The following reflections are intended to help Catholic schools on all levels, including seminaries and universities, to implement the mandate of the Holy See's 1998 statement *We Remember: A Reflection on the Shoah.*[1] These reflections do not in themselves form a curriculum but rather are designed to help Catholic educators begin developing curricula and other educational programs on the Holocaust.

The process used to develop this document may in itself serve as a model for local diocesan and Catholic schools seeking to implement the Holy See's charge to grapple with the implications of the *Shoah* for the Church itself. In early 1999 the Bishops' Committee for Ecumenical and Interreligious Relations (BCEIA) joined with the American Jewish Committee and the Archdiocese of Baltimore to cosponsor a dialogue of leading Catholic and Jewish educators. These teachers, fifteen from each community, some of whom are pioneers in the field, had all been involved in Holocaust education for many years. Early drafts, in turn, were shown to an even wider group of Jewish and Catholic educators and then were discussed and reframed by ourselves at our meetings before they were formally adopted. We hope, then, that they reflect the experience and wisdom of the educators whose intense dialogue raised the issues they confront, as well as the pastoral sense we brought to the issues as bishops.

WHY DO CATHOLICS STUDY THE *SHOAH*?

The *Shoah* can briefly be described as Nazi Germany's systematic and nearly successful attempt, from its foreshadowing on *Kristallnacht* in 1938 to its actual implementation from 1942 to 1945, to murder every Jewish woman, man, and child in Europe. By the end, two out of every three members of the ancient European Jewish community had been killed—some six million people—along with millions of Gypsies (Romani), homosexuals, Poles, and other "sub-humans" *(untermenschen)*. So horrendous was this mass killing that the Church at the end of the twentieth century (which Pope John Paul II has not hesitated to call "the Century of the *Shoah*"),[2] has in *We Remember* called on its members collectively to repent not only for their sins of omission and commission during the *Shoah*, but also for the many centuries of negative teachings about Jews and Judaism that, in the pope's words, so "lulled the consciences" of so many European Christians that they were not able to organize an effective resistance to Nazi genocide:[3]

> At the end of this millennium the Catholic Church desires to express her deep sorrow for the failures of her sons and daughters in every age. This is an act of repentance (*teshuvah*), since as members of the Church we are linked to the sins as well as the merits of all her children. The Church approaches with deep respect and great compassion the experience of extermination, the *Shoah* suffered by the Jewish people during World War II. It is not a matter of mere words, but indeed of binding commitment. . . . We pray that our sorrow for the tragedy which the Jewish people has suffered in our century will lead to a new relationship with the Jewish people. We wish to turn awareness of past sins into a firm resolve to build a new future in which there will be no more anti-Judaism among Christians . . . but rather a shared mutual respect as befits those who adore the one Creator and Lord and have a common father in faith, Abraham.[4]

The pope and the Holy See here distill the essential and overriding reasons for Catholic education to grapple with the *Shoah* as part of its central curriculum. First, the *Shoah* was neither a random act of mass murder nor simply the result of a war or ancient enmity between two peoples (as most other genocides have been). It was a war against the Jews as the People of God, the First Witnesses to God's Revelation and the eternal bearers of that witness through all the centuries since. It is not accidental that the first direct physical attack on the Jews, *Kristallnacht*, came in 1938 in the form of the burning of synagogues throughout the Nazi-dominated parts of Europe. To create its Third Reich, conceived as a millennium of Aryan domination over the entire earth, the Nazi regime, in its ideology, quite rightly saw that it would have to destroy all memory of divine revelation by destroying first the Jews and then the Church. Only by eliminating the moral inhibitions of Judaism and Christianity from the European conscience would Nazism be able to recreate humanity in its own warped racist image and likeness.

The second reason to include the *Shoah* in Catholic education is that the Church today, speaking for and to all Catholics, needs to remind future generations to be ever-vigilant so that "the spoiled seeds of anti-Judaism and antisemitism [will] never again be allowed to take root in any human heart."[5] These underlying mandates of *We Remember* can be set down as educational goals as follows, noting of course that in specific circumstances other articulations and emphases may be appropriate.

GOALS FOR *SHOAH* EDUCATION IN A CATHOLIC CONTEXT

1. To provide Catholics with accurate knowledge of and respect for Judaism, the eternal covenant between God and the Jewish People, and the spiritual bond of kinship between Jews and Christians.[6] Accomplishing this goal educationally will involve students in "learn[ing] by what essential traits the Jews define themselves in the light of their own religious experience."[7]

2. To encourage a positive appreciation of Jews and Judaism and the ongoing role of the Jewish People in God's plan of salvation. This role, the Church teaches, was not exhausted in preparing the way for and giving birth to Jesus. It will continue until the end of time. Thus, Pope John Paul II has spoken of the Church and the Jewish people as being joint "trustees and witnesses of an ethic," and of "our common heritage drawn from the Law and the Prophets." Our joint witness with Jews to the world, the pope concludes, should be "marked by the Ten Commandments, in the observance of which [humanity] finds [its] truth and freedom."[8] Likewise, the pope has spoken of the need for joint Catholic-Jewish witness to the memory of the *Shoah*.[9]

3. To promote the spirit of repentance and conversion called for by *We Remember* and integral to the observance of Jubilee 2000 and beyond.[10] In particular, Catholic institutions of higher learning are called to study "the fact that the *Shoah* took place in Europe, that is, in countries of long-standing Christian civilization, [which] raises the question of the relation between the Nazi persecution and the attitudes down the centuries of Christians toward Jews."[11]

4. To arm Catholics for the ongoing fight against traditional Christian anti-Judaism and modern racial antisemitism, by studying the causes and

conditions for genocide in order to prevent such atrocities from happening to Jews or any other group in the future.[12] Study of the *Shoah* demonstrates vividly to what lengths of destruction prejudice, whether religious or secular in origin, can lead.

FRAMING ISSUES PROPERLY AND SENSITIVELY

The *Shoah* was a complex event that took place within the context of the most widespread and destructive war humanity has ever known. As Archbishop Alexander Brunett explains in his introduction to *Catholics Remember the Holocaust*,

> [Fr.] John Hotchkin [director of the Secretariat for Ecumenical and Interreligious Affairs] observed that the chillingly systematic effort to exterminate an entire people, not for what they had done nor for any threat they posed, but simply for being who they were—whether young or old; every last man, woman, and child— is an attempt at evil on a nearly unimaginable scale. Thus, the *Shoah* raises in a most awful way the darkest questions the mystery of evil has put to the human family in our time. We may never get to the bottom of these questions. For something this evil there is in the end no explanation the mind can accept. It remains a dark and threatening mystery. But what we cannot explain, we must nevertheless remember. The warning contained in the memory is our best common shield and defense. The evil that turns humanity against humanity, cheapening its life, degrading it, bent on its destruction, still lurks in the world. It does not rest and neither must we in our remembering, for it is by remembering the unspeakable horror that did in fact happen that we remain awake and alert to the possibility that what happened could be attempted again. It is through our common remembrance of those who perished that they shield the living. This is a cataclysm unlike any other in human history. Indeed, the theologian David Tracy has written of it as an "interruption" of history, an event in which "our history crashes against itself." It is as if time stopped, and history thereafter could never again be the same. For this reason it is imperative that the memory be kept and the story be told from generation to generation.[13]

The issues need to be framed for Catholic students with care and concern. On the one hand, as we have seen, this catastrophe was so unprecedented that many people, whether Jews or Christians, found the very fact of it hard to comprehend until it was too late to oppose. On the other hand, many people, Jews and Christians, did sense what was at stake and fought against it. The role of these "righteous," the rescuers, when placed in a proper, subordinated perspective, will provide a necessary model for future generations.

Similarly, because of the *Shoah's* unprecedented nature, a new word, "genocide," had to be invented to describe it. But once invented, "genocide" can justly be applied to other victims of the Nazis, such as Gypsies and Poles, and to other events in this century, such as mass murders in Asia, Africa, and Europe. The similarities and differences between these phenomena can fruitfully be explored and analyzed in the classroom.

In confronting the *Shoah*, honesty and objectivity are vital tools for educators, especially when dealing with matters that may appear unfavorable to Christians or to the Church. Pope John Paul II reminded Catholic scholars who were gathered at the Vatican to study "The Roots of Anti-Judaism in the Christian Milieu" on October 31, 1997: "I appreciate the fact that the theological research conducted by your symposium is done with scholarly rigor, in the conviction that to serve the truth is to serve Christ himself and his church."

At the same time, the chaotic and intimidating situation faced by ordinary people caught up in a conflagration of unprecedented scope will need to be taken into account by educators. Situations varied tremendously from one area of Europe to another. The Nazis treated local populations differently according to their places on the racial ladder. Slavs, being in Nazi eyes less than fully human, were considered fit only to be slaves, while Danes were seen as fellow Aryans who might have a place in the Nazi millennium. In Poland alone it was a capital offense to aid a Jew in any way. Whole families and entire Polish villages were murdered by the Nazis for harboring Jews, and a Pole could be killed even for offering a Jew a crust of bread.

In some countries, such as Italy, Denmark, and Bulgaria, virtually the entire population rose to the occasion to save the lives of their fellow citizens of Jewish birth. In others, such as France and Austria, heroic resistance and craven collaboration coexisted. In such a complex situation, few generalities can be made about historical precedents, perpetrators, bystanders, rescuers, and ordinary people. The following sections raise two issues about which particular care is needed: presenting the stories of the Rescuers and the importance of making proper distinctions.

THE RESCUERS

Israel's major Holocaust museum, Yad Vashem in Jerusalem, remembers and honors the "righteous gentiles" who risked their own lives to save Jews. The U.S. Holocaust Memorial Museum in Washington, D.C., similarly honors them, not only listing the names of individuals but offering special exhibits on countries such as Denmark and Italy, each of which saved over 80 percent of the Jews of their countries, and on groups such as Zegota, a Polish Catholic organization dedicated to saving Jewish lives.

Again, a sense of balance is needed. Cardinal William H. Keeler of Baltimore, in an address honoring Catholic rescuers at the U.S. Holocaust Memorial Museum in April 1997, placed the occasion firmly within the context of the overall need for repentance on the part of Catholics worldwide, as called for by the pope and the Holy See. The rescuers were, after all, relatively few islands of light in a continent overwhelmed by the darkness of evil. Still, the rescuers remain crucial models for future generations of Catholics. Studies have revealed some widespread characteristics of rescuers that can be inculcated educationally.

First, a sense of morality was deeply implanted in the fiber of their being, whether they were sophisticated and well educated or ordinary people. Rescuers frequently had to make life-or-death decisions (not only for themselves but for their families) on short notice. Most in postwar interviews have said that they felt they had little choice. They could only do "what was right," thus exhibiting a reflex toward the good, often enough despite full awareness of the risks involved.

Second, the righteous had a sense that life has ultimate meaning beyond the present. While their understanding of that meaning may have varied, their experience reminds us to place our lives in a wider context of human meaning and interrelatedness. For Catholics this sense of openness to the transcendent dimension underscores the critical importance of faith in God.

Third, many of the righteous had prior acquaintance with Jews, though not necessarily with the people they actually rescued. From this we learn the importance of building human bonds across religious, racial, and ethnic lines.

DISTINCTIONS AND CONNECTIONS: THEOLOGICAL AND HISTORICAL

The essence of a good education may lie in developing the skills necessary to make proper distinctions and connections among related phenomena. In this way biology distinguishes and relates the wealth of the world's flora and fauna by classifying them into genus and species in order to understand how life on earth "works." The same is true of theology and the social sciences.

Some responses, Catholic as well as Jewish, to *We Remember* questioned certain distinctions made by the Holy See's commission. These, however, flow from the Church's traditional understanding of itself as a divinely founded institution, and from a careful consideration of history. The chief signer of the document, Cardinal Edward I. Cassidy, clarified what was meant at a meeting with the American Jewish Committee in May 1998.[14] The pope's liturgy of repentance at St. Peter's in Rome in March 2000, his statement the following week at Yad Vashem, and the petition for forgiveness that he placed, in the name of the whole Church, in the Western Wall (*Kotel*) in Jerusalem all presume these distinctions. Properly interpreted, the distinctions made by the Holy See are crucial to Catholic *Shoah* education. They are elaborated upon at some length in the statement of the Vatican's International Theological Commission, *Memory and Reconciliation: The Church and Faults of the Past,* issued on Ash Wednesday of the Jubilee Year 2000 in order to explain the precise meaning of the pope's Liturgy of Repentance on the First Sunday of Lent that year.[15]

The Church, Its Members, and Responsibility for the *Shoah*

The distinction made by the documents between "the Church as such" and "her sons and daughters" is a traditional one, familiar to most Catholics. No one—not popes or bishops or priests or laity—is exempt from sin, as Cardinal Cassidy explained. Thus the petition for forgiveness that Pope John Paul II placed in the Western Wall prayed to the "God of our fathers" in the name of the whole Church. The pope did not mean to exclude anyone by reason of rank or clerical status from responsibility for their acts toward Jews over the centuries: "We are deeply saddened / by the behavior of those / who in the course of history / have caused these children of yours to suffer." This statement of repentance at the Wall, coming just after the pope's prayerful visit to Yad Vashem, includes the sins of omission and commission by Catholics toward Jews both in the centuries leading up to the *Shoah* and during it.

At the same time, the Church is more than a human institution. It is the Body of Christ incarnate in the world after his Ascension into heaven, the sacrament of the encounter between the divine and the human, the sure instrument of salvation offered to all humanity. *Memory and Reconciliation,* referring to Augustine and Thomas Aquinas, notes the seeming paradox that the Church is at once indefectibly holy and in need of "continual renewal" through repentance,[16] and the statement makes clear that "the fullness of holiness belongs to eschatological time; in the meantime, the church still on pilgrimage should not deceive herself by saying that she is without sin."[17]

These paired theological affirmations, we believe, take on particular urgency when applied to Christian-Jewish relations over the centuries and especially during the Holocaust. The polemical teachings of the Church Fathers against Judaism that began in the second century (as the pope noted in 1997) and the severe persecutions of Jews that so marred the second millennium were so pervasive over time that the consciences of twentieth-century Christians were "lulled." The result was that a continent, "Christian" for centuries, found all too few Christians capable of resisting the virus of racial antisemitism propagated by Nazism. A few did, and their heroism in saving Jewish lives is a model for students today. But many more did not, and for this the Church as a whole, in the moving phrases of Pope John Paul II and of *We Remember,* must repent and take responsibility. As *We Remember* puts it so well: "At the end of this millennium the Catholic Church desires to express her deep sorrow for the failures of her sons and daughters in every age. This is an act of repentance *(teshuvah)*, since as members of the Church we are linked to the sins as well as the merits of all her children."[18]

Anti-Judaism and Antisemitism
We Remember distinguishes broadly between the theological polemics against Judaism developed by Christian teachers as early as the second century and the more modern racial and neo-pagan ideology of antisemitism that was developed in the eighteenth and nineteenth centuries to euphemize racial hatred

directed against Jews. Again, the distinction is crucial to understanding. The classic Christian approach to Judaism, as formulated by St. Augustine and set into lasting canonical precedent by Pope St. Gregory the Great, was fundamentally ambiguous in theory and practice. On the one hand, Jews were considered "blind" to the true meaning of their own Scriptures, not seeing their fulfillment in Christ. But their witness to the validity of the Hebrew Bible as divine revelation was seen as essential to the witness of the Church to Christ. Hence, Jews were to be allowed to worship (relatively) freely and were not to be forced to convert to Christianity. Judaism was thus the only licit religion besides Christianity in Christendom throughout the Middle Ages. The popes could be and often were successfully appealed to by Jewish communities when local civil authorities attempted to abuse them.

What specifically Christian anti-Judaism led to when it was abused was forced conversion; occasional, mindless massacres like those of the Crusaders in 1096; expulsion by secular rulers (beginning with England in the twelfth century and culminating in the 1492 expulsion from Spain); and the ghettoization of the remaining Jews of Western Europe.[19] These Christian sins are indefensible. But when the Church was able to exercise authority in the civil societies of Europe (i.e., from the fourth century to the Enlightenment), the moral teaching of Church law acted at times as a restraint. At no time did the plight of Jews degenerate into anything near the systematic attempt at genocide that was the direct result of the adoption of a neo-pagan set of racial ideologies by the Nazi Reich in Germany. This total dehumanization of Jews allowed those who adopted it to conceive and implement the "final solution" for ridding Europe of the "infestation" of its Jewish population.

But Christian anti-Judaism did lay the groundwork for racial, genocidal anti-semitism by stigmatizing not only Judaism but Jews themselves for opprobrium and contempt. So the Nazi theories tragically found fertile soil in which to plant the horror of an unprecedented attempt at genocide. One way to put the "connectedness" between the Christian teaching of anti-Judaism (leading to anti-Jewishness) and Nazi antisemitism is that the former is a "necessary cause" to consider in explaining the development and success of the latter in the twentieth century—but not a "sufficient cause." To account for the Holocaust, one must acknowledge the historical role of Christian anti-Judaism. But Christian anti-Judaism alone cannot account for the Holocaust. Semi-scientific racial theories and specific historical, ideological, economic, and social realities within Germany must also be taken into account in order to begin grappling with why Nazism succeeded in mobilizing virtually the entire intellectual and technological apparatus of a modern industrial state to its warped purpose of eliminating from human history God's People, the Jews.

Guilt and Responsibility

It may be necessary to explain to students that the universal call to repentance before God for Christian sins against Jews that the Holy Father mandated during the Jubilee Year 2000, as well as *We Remember*'s call for the Church's ongoing repentance for these sins, will involve for most Christians an assumption of responsibility for our collective Christian past, not personal guilt. Moral guilt—and it must be remembered that antisemitism is and was a most serious sin—inheres only in the sinner. It cannot be passed on to others. Americans in the generation of Nazi tyranny in Europe fought to defeat it, although our refusal to let in more than a handful of the Jewish refugees should give us reason to examine our national conscience as well.[20] In any event, those born after the war have no reason to feel personal guilt; but members of the one Body of Christ, the Church, have every reason to assume responsibility to ensure that nothing like it can ever happen again.

The Holy See's *Memory and Reconciliation* takes up this issue in some depth, pointing to the biblical writers' "strong sense of solidarity in good and evil among the generations" ("corporate personality") as the model for us today: "This is how the Jews prayed after the exile [*Daniel* 3:26-30; *Baruch* 2:11-13], accepting the responsibility for the sins committed by their fathers. The church imitates their example and also asks forgiveness for the historical sins of her children."[21]

Again, *We Remember* says well what needs to be said: "It is not a matter of mere words, but indeed of binding commitment. . . . We wish to turn awareness of past sins into a firm resolve to build a new future in which there will be no more anti-Judaism among Christians."[22]

SUGGESTIONS FOR TEACHING COURSES ON THE *SHOAH*

The course should fit into the mission of the particular Catholic school or program developing it. Courses offered in Catholic universities, theological schools, and seminaries, for example, will engage the students and faculty in complex theological issues regarding the Church as a whole and its understanding of Scripture, ecclesiology, and especially the liturgy, while courses on the elementary level might focus more helpfully on individual narratives of victims and rescuers, bringing out the moral implications in order to prepare students to be morally grounded leaders for tomorrow. The *Shoah* destroyed a vibrant culture along with innumerable institutions of higher learning, especially religious learning. Courses, as the outline below suggests, should include some history of Jewish thought, devotion, and culture.

Many fields of study are relevant to *Shoah* education, ranging from history, psychology, and sociology to philosophy, theology, and the arts. Team-taught, interdisciplinary, and interreligious (led by a Catholic and a Jewish teacher) approaches have much to recommend them in a given academic context.

Since it is impossible to teach all aspects of the *Shoah* in a single semester, goals will need to be prioritized depending on resources available to the school and in the community. For example, in Washington, D.C., the archdiocese has been able to draw on the expertise of the U.S. Holocaust Memorial Museum and the Anti-Defamation League to develop an annual summer program that has trained, as of 1999, some 240 Catholic secondary teachers from various departments in Holocaust education. Some schools and school systems, like Georgetown Preparatory School in the District of Columbia and the public schools of New Jersey, have developed cyclical curricula in which successive years build on the year before. An innovative educational program, "Facing History and Ourselves," began in Boston and is now used in public and parochial schools throughout the country. The National Catholic Center for Holocaust Education at Seton Hill College in Greensburg, Pennsylvania, can be a vital resource for diocesan programming. Below is a list of some of the topics that might be covered in such Holocaust education programs.

Prior History of Jewish-Christian Relations

1. Pre-Christian antipathy to Jews

2. Origins and development of the Christian teaching of contempt for Jews and Judaism, and the papal and canonical legislation that nevertheless offered Jews a legal place in Christian society and often sought to protect them from exploitation by civil leaders

3. Spiritual and intellectual creativity of post-New Testament Jewish history (Talmud, Maimonides, Rashi, mysticism, etc.) and its contributions to Western civilization

4. Marginalization and demonization of Jews in Christendom

5. Racial antisemitism—distinct in theory and ideology, but historically and socially connected to Christian theological anti-Judaism

General Preconditions
1. Technological change

2. Economic and political instability

3. Secularized society (and the diminution of Christian moral restraints on certain actions)

Events of the *Shoah* Itself
1. Basic history, including the destruction of a vital culture

2. Jewish and non-Jewish victims of Nazism

3. Perpetrators, bystanders, beneficiaries, and average citizens—some whom were led by their own apathy to turn their heads away, while others may have harbored fears for their own families that led them to be silent bystanders

4. Resisters and rescuers

5. Roles and responses of Catholic, Protestant, and Orthodox Churches and how they varied from country to country, region to region

6. Roles and responses of various Christian international bodies, especially the Holy See and the World Council of Churches, and of other international agencies, such as the Red Cross

Aftermath of the *Shoah*: Efforts to Respond
1. Jewish responses: theological challenges, State of Israel, creation of memory

2. Christian responses: e.g., the Second Vatican Council twenty years after the event, though issues had been raised by individual Protestants and Catholics sooner, such as facing the history of the "teaching of contempt," replacement theology (supersessionism), challenges to internal theological

issues (e.g., teachings about Christian love, value of life), theological methodologies and Christian worship (e.g., *God's Mercy Endures Forever*)

3. Moral implications for our world: responses to genocide, prejudice, and antisemitism in its various forms, including in international relations

4. General challenge to our conceptions of Western civilization, including liberal learning, academia, and the professions

5. Challenges raised in remembering and canonizing individuals from the time of the *Shoah*, questions of biography and hagiography (e.g., Lichtenberg, Kolbe, Stein, Titus Brandsma)[23]

PEDAGOGICAL ISSUES

Experiential Aspects
It is beneficial to use film, testimonies (of survivors, rescuers, liberators, and children of survivors), literature, Internet resources, and/or museum visits to engage students affectively in their studies. Care must be taken not to horrify younger students to the point that they are desensitized or refuse to relate to the issues. Sensitivity to the feelings of guilt or victimization that can arise is imperative.

Contextual Issues
1. The *Shoah* should not be the only context in which Jews and Judaism are encountered in a curriculum. Even within a *Shoah* course, Jews and Judaism should not be encountered only as the *Shoah*'s victims or as perennial scapegoats of Christian persecutions.

2. The *Shoah* must also be confronted within various contexts of general European history, especially of Germany and Austria, but also of all the other countries in which the Nazis were able to operate. The differences between these contexts need to be brought out.

Construction of Memory
1. The instructor should be conscious of the moral imperative to construct a memory of the *Shoah* that will positively influence the moral formation of students. In a Catholic setting, students should come to accept and regret that the perpetrators, bystanders, and the cowed majority in Europe came from within the Christian community. Similarly, Jewish students should

come to identify with the victims. Both Catholic and Jewish students should also learn something about the more positive relations between Jews and Catholics as fellow immigrants in America. The need to create this memory and identification should shape the structure of the course. The formation of an empathetic imagination for the memories and sensibilities of others should also be pursued.

2. Students must be conscious that this construction of memory is different depending on the person's entry into identification (positive or negative) with the people involved in the *Shoah*. They should be aware that the memory of the *Shoah* for Jews is necessarily a radically different memory from that of most Christians. The distinctive victimization of such groups as Poles and other Slavs, gypsies, homosexuals, and the physically or mentally impaired also has an impact on the construction of memory of individual students.

3. While the *Shoah* was in many respects a unique event, victims of the all-too-numerous other incidents of mass murder will find analytical distinctions trivial to their experience of suffering.

BEYOND COURSES ON THE *SHOAH*

The issues of the *Shoah* and of Jewish-Christian relations are vast topics that most students will encounter only as elective offerings in their total programs of study. Yet their enormous importance requires their integration wherever possible throughout the Catholic curricula. This is especially, though not solely, important for seminaries and theological schools. In biblical studies, for example, courses on books of the Shared Testament (Hebrew Scriptures) should convey esteem for the profundity and permanence of Israel's experience of God and its inspired sacred texts. Courses on the New Testament will benefit from taking seriously the Jewishness of Jesus and the Apostles, and of the Evangelists, Paul, and other authors of the New Testament. Preachers can help improve future sermons and Catholic texts by confronting honestly the anti-Jewish potential of certain passages, especially those concerning the crucifixion, the Pharisees, the Torah (Law), and the permanence of Israel's covenant.[24] Christological courses will be enriched by accurately reflecting the complexities of Judaism in late antiquity as the context of Jesus' teaching and of the early Church's understanding of the significance of the Christ event.

In courses in patristic studies, the pervasive—and now repudiated—idea that Christianity replaced or "superseded" Judaism in God's plan of salvation needs to be challenged. Here, it is worthy of note: "It has rightly been stressed that of all the documents promulgated by the Second Vatican Council, that on the Jews [*Nostra Aetate*] is the only one which contains no reference whatsoever to any of the Church's teachings—patristic, conciliar or pontifical. This alone shows the revolutionary character of the act."[25] Courses on church history and European history will benefit greatly when taught from the vantage point of the perennially marginalized Jewish community, the only religious tradition in Europe that pre-dated Christianity and still exists intact and in continuity with its past.

Homiletics courses and courses devoted to the Rite of Christian Initiation of Adults can explore the relationship between the two testaments of the Christian Bible so as to avoid presentations that explicitly or subtly promote supersessionism. Ethics courses can examine the situations and behaviors of the churches during the *Shoah* and benefit from the "double lens" of how Christians and Jews over the centuries have variously interpreted the moral commandments of the Scriptures we share.

To understand the liturgical renewal of the twentieth century and the origins of much that is central to Christian practice, the Jewish roots of our forms of worship need to be understood. Spirituality courses can treat the writings of Jewish commentators and mystics.

These issues need to be integrated into other parts of the daily life of Catholic educational institutions through special events such as commemorations of *Yom HaShoah* (the Jewish day of remembering the victims of the Holocaust), film showings, drama, art exhibits, colloquia and public lectures, joint pilgrimages and retreats with Jewish clergy and laity, and faculty and student exchanges like the American Jewish Committee's CJEEP (Catholic-Jewish Educational Exchange Program).

NOTES

1. Similarly, the Bishops' Committee for Ecumenical and Interreligious Relations (BCEIA) sought to implement locally the Holy See's statements of 1974 and 1985 with the 1975 NCCB *Statement on Catholic-Jewish Relations* and our own 1988 *Criteria for the Evaluation of Dramatizations of the Passion* (Washington, D.C.: United

States Catholic Conference). The Bishops' Committee on the Liturgy further drew out the liturgical implications of the Holy See's 1985 statement in its own statement, *God's Mercy Endures Forever: Guidelines on the Presentation of Jews and Judaism in Catholic Preaching* (Washington, D.C.: United States Catholic Conference, 1989). The Holy See's 1998 statement *We Remember*, along with related statements of European and U.S. bishops' conferences, is contained in *Catholics Remember the Holocaust* (Washington, D.C.: United States Catholic Conference, 1998). In *We Remember*, the Holy See wisely uses the Hebrew word *Shoah* to describe the Holocaust. While not diminishing the suffering of Nazism's many other victims, such as the Romani (Gypsies) and Poles, this term preserves a central focus on Nazism's central victim-group, God's People, the Jews. The present reflection follows this precedent.

2. John Paul II's Address to the Jewish Community of Australia, November 26, 1986. This and other papal texts on Jews and Judaism between 1979 and 1995 can be found, with introduction and commentary, in John Paul II, *Spiritual Pilgrimage: Texts on Jews and Judaism*, eds. Eugene Fisher and Leon Klenicki (New York: Crossroad, 1995).

3. John Paul II, Speech to Symposium on the Roots of Anti-Judaism, October 31, 1997. *L'Osservatore Romano* 6:1 (November 6, 1997).

4. *We Remember*, Part 5. In *Catholics Remember the Holocaust,* p. 54. On the distinction between anti-Judaism and antisemitism, see Part 4.

5. Ibid., p. 55.

6. In a 1985 statement, the Vatican's Commission for Religious Relations with the Jews had this to say regarding Catholic teachings on Judaism: "The urgency and importance of precise, objective and rigorously accurate teaching on Judaism for our faithful follows too from the danger of anti-semitism which is always ready to reappear under different guises. The question is not merely to uproot from among the faithful the remains of anti-semitism still to be found here and there, but much rather to arouse in them, through educational work, an exact knowledge of the wholly unique 'bond' (*Nostra Aetate*, 4) which joins us as a Church to the Jews and to Judaism." *Notes on the Correct Way to Present the Jews and Judaism in Preaching and Catechesis in the Roman Catholic Church* (June 24, 1985), section 1, no. 8. In *Catholic Jewish Relations: Documents from the Holy See* (London: Catholic Truth Society, 1999).

7. Vatican Commission for Religious Relations with the Jews, *Guidelines and Suggestions for Implementing of the Conciliar Declaration Nostra Aetate, no. 4* (December 1, 1974), preamble. In *Catholic Jewish Relations*.

8. John Paul II, Address in the Great Synagogue of Rome (April 13, 1986), no. 6. In *Spiritual Pilgrimage*, p. 65.

9. Addressing the Jewish leaders of Warsaw on June 14, 1987, the Holy Father expanded his vision of ongoing Jewish witness to include the *Shoah* itself: "I think that today . . . you have become a loud warning voice for all humanity. . . . More

than anyone else, it is precisely you who have become this saving warning. . . . in this sense you continue your particular vocation, showing yourselves to be still the heirs of that election to which God is faithful. This is your mission in the contemporary world before the peoples, the nations, all of humanity, the Church. And in this Church all peoples and nations feel united to you in this mission." In *Spiritual Pilgrimage*, p. 99.

10. John Paul II, *On the Coming of the Third Millennium (Tertio Millennio Adveniente)*, no. 33 (Washington, D.C.: United States Catholic Conference, 1994).

11. *We Remember,* part 2. In *Catholics Remember the Holocaust,* p. 49.

12. "We would risk causing the victims of the most atrocious deaths to die again if we do not have an ardent desire for justice, if we do not commit ourselves to ensure that evil does not prevail over good as it did for millions of the children of the Jewish people. . . Humanity cannot permit all that to happen again." *We Remember,* part 5, citing John Paul II. In *Catholics Remember the Holocaust,* p. 55.

13. *Catholics Remember the Holocaust,* p. 2.

14. The text of Cardinal Cassidy's "Reflections Regarding the Vatican's Statement on the *Shoah*," originally published in *Origins,* is included in *Catholics Remember the Holocaust,* pp. 61-76.

15. International Theological Commission, *Memory and Reconciliation: The Church and the Faults of the Past,* in *Origins* 29:39 (March 16, 2000): 625-644.

16. Ibid., no. 3.3.

17. Ibid.

18. *We Remember,* part 5. In *Catholics Remember the Holocaust,* p. 54. See also *Memory and Reconciliation,* nos. 3.4 and 5.4.

19. It should be noted that Jews were never expelled from Italy, where papal authority continued the tradition of protection of Jews. Likewise, many Jews found refuge in Eastern Europe, especially Poland, which by the twentieth century enjoyed the largest Jewish population in the world.

20. See Archbishop Oscar Lipscomb (BCEIA chairman) "Commemorating the [50th Anniversary of the] Liberation of Auschwitz." In *Catholics Remember the Holocaust,* pp. 16-20.

21. *Memory and Reconciliation,* no. 2.1.

22. *We Remember,* part 5. In *Catholics Remember the Holocaust,* p. 54.

23. Cf. Cardinal William H. Keeler, "Lessons to Learn from Catholic Rescuers." In *Catholics Remember the Holocaust,* pp. 29-30.

24. See *God's Mercy Endures Forever.*

25. Gerhart M. Riegner, *Nostra Aetate: Twenty Years After.* In International Catholic-Jewish Liaison Committee, *Fifteen Years of Catholic-Jewish Dialogue, 1970-1985: Selected Papers,* p. 276 (Vatican City: Libreria Editrice Vaticana, 1988).

Bibliography of Resources

HISTORICAL DOCUMENTATION AND CHURCH TEACHINGS

Blet, Pierre. *Pius XII and the Second World War: According the Archives of the Vatican.* New York: Paulist Press, 1999. Survey of the documentation made available by the Holy See, and a gripping, virtually day-by-day narrative of how it reacted to the events of the war and of the *Shoah*.

Blet, Pierre, Angelo Martini, and Burkhart Schneider, eds. *Actes et documents du Saint Siège relatifs à la Seconde Guerre mondiale.* Libreria Editrice Vaticana, 1965-80. Eleven volumes of documentation.

Fisher, Eugene J. *Faith Without Prejudice: Rebuilding Christian Attitudes Toward Judaism.* New York: Crossroad, 1993.

Fisher, Eugene J., and Leon Klenicki, eds. *Spiritual Pilgrimage: Texts on Jews and Judaism 1979-1995.* New York: Crossroad, 1995.

———. *In Our Age: The Flowering of Jewish-Catholic Dialogue.* New York: Paulist Press, 1990. Provides texts and commentary on the statements of the Holy See from the 1965 declaration of the Second Vatican Council to 1986. For texts up to 1998, see *Catholic Jewish Relations: Documents from the Holy See* (London: Catholic Truth Society, 1999).

International Theological Commission of the Holy See. *Memory and Reconciliation: The Church and Faults of the Past.* March 8, 2000. *Origins* 29:39 (March 16, 2000): 625-644.

Secretariat for Ecumenical and Interreligious Affairs, National Conference of Catholic Bishops. *Catholics Remember the Holocaust.* Washington, D.C.: United States Catholic Conference, 1998. Contains statements on the *Shoah* by the Vatican and the episcopal conferences in Europe and the United States.

ON *SHOAH* EDUCATION

Garber, Zev, and Richard Libowitz, eds. *Peace, in Deed: Essays in Honor of Harry James Cargas.* Atlanta: Scholars Press, 1998.

Garber, Zev, Alan L. Berger, and Richard Libowitz, eds. *Methodology in the Academic Teaching of the Holocaust.* Lanham, Md.: University Press of America, 1988. Seventeen essays on theory and methods, teaching others, literature and arts, and surveys and reports.

Haynes, Stephen R. *Holocaust Education and the Church-Related College: Restoring Ruptured Traditions.* Westport, Conn.: Greenwood Press, 1997. Critical reflection on the state of Holocaust education in Protestant-related settings, its mandates, and its challenges.

Millen, Rochelle L., et al., eds. *New Perspectives on the Holocaust: A Guide for Teachers and Scholars.* New York: New York University Press, 1996. Twenty-five essays on the context of the Holocaust, issues of teaching and curriculum, and spiritual and moral issues.

Napolitano, Daniel C. *The Holocaust: A Teaching Guide for Catholic Schools.* Washington, D.C.: U.S. Holocaust Memorial Museum, 1999.

Shimoni, Gideon, ed. *The Holocaust in University Teaching.* New York: Pergamon Press, 1991. Four methodological articles and twenty-six syllabi, heavily drawn from Jewish faculty.

THE *SHOAH* AND RELIGIOUS REFLECTION

Berenbaum, Michael. *After Tragedy and Triumph: Essays in Modern Jewish Thought and the American Experience.* New York: Cambridge University Press, 1990.

————. *Elie Wiesel, God, the Holocaust, and the Children of Israel.* West Orange, N.J.: Behrman House, 1994.

————. *The Vision of the Void: Theological Reflections on the Works of Elie Wiesel.* Middletown, Conn.: Wesleyan University Press, 1979.

————, ed. *A Mosaic of Victims: Non-Jews Persecuted and Murdered by the Nazis.* New York: New York University Press, 1990.

Brenner, Reeve Robert. *The Faith and Doubt of Holocaust Survivors.* New York: Free Press, 1980.

Brown, Robert McAfee. *Elie Wiesel, Messenger to All Humanity.* Rev. ed. Notre Dame, Ind.: University of Notre Dame, 1989.

Eckardt, A. Roy, and Alice L. Eckardt. *Long Night's Journey into Day: Life and Faith After the Holocaust.* Detroit: Wayne State University Press, 1982.

Fiorenza, Elisabeth Schüssler, and David Tracy, eds. *The Holocaust as Interruption: A Quest for Christian Theology.* Edinburgh: T. & T. Clark, 1984.

Fleischner, Eva, ed. *Auschwitz: Beginning of a New Era?: Reflections on the Holocaust.* New York: Ktav Publishing Co., 1977.

Garber, Zev. *Shoah: The Paradigmatic Genocide.* Lanham, Md.: University Press of America, 1994.

Jacobs, Steven L., ed. *The Holocaust Now: Contemporary Christian and Jewish Thought.* East Rockaway, N.Y.: Cummings & Hathaway, 1996.

Littell, Franklin H. *The Crucifixion of the Jews.* New York: Harper & Row, 1975.

Littell, Franklin H., and Hubert G. Locke, eds. *The German Church Struggle and the Holocaust.* Detroit: Wayne State University Press, 1974.

Littel, Marcia Sachs, and Sharon Weissman Gutman. *Liturgies on the Holocaust: An Interfaith Anthology.* New and rev. ed. Valley Forge, Penn.: Trinity Press International, 1996.

Morley, John I. *Vatican Diplomacy and the Jews During the Holocaust, 1939-1943.* New York: Ktav Publishing Co., 1980.

Peck, Abraham J., ed. *Jews and Christians After the Holocaust.* Philadelphia: Fortress, 1982.

Rittner, Carol, and John K. Roth. *From the Unthinkable to the Unknowable: American Christian and Jewish Scholars Encounter the Holocaust.* Westport, Conn.: Praeger, 1997.

Roth, John, and Michael Berenbaum, eds. *Holocaust: Religious and Philosophical Implications.* New York: Paragon House, 1989.

Schulweis, Harold M. "A Jewish Theology for Post-Holocaust Healing." *Midstream* (August/September 1987): 44-46.

Wiesenthal, Simon. *The Sunflower: On the Possibilities and Limits of Forgiveness.* Rev. ed. New York: Schocken, 1998.

RESCUERS

Axelrod, Toby. *Rescuers Defying the Nazis: Non-Jewish Teens Who Rescued Jews.* New York: Rosen, 1999.

Bartoszewski, Wladyslaw, and Zofia Lewin, eds. *Righteous Among Nations: How Poles Helped the Jews, 1939-1945.* London: Earlscourt Publications, 1969.

Fisher, Eugene J. "Faith in Humankind: Rescuers of Jews in the Holocaust." *Journal of Ecumenical Studies* 21 (1984): 636-637.

Fogelman, Eva. *Conscience and Courage: Rescuers of Jews During the Holocaust.* New York: Anchor Books, 1994.

Friedman, Philip. *Their Brothers' Keepers.* New York: Holocaust Library, 1978.

Gies, Miep, and Alison Leslie Gold. *Anne Frank Remembered: The Story of the Woman Who Helped to Hide the Frank Family.* New York: Simon & Schuster, 1987.

Gushee, David P. *The Righteous Gentiles of the Holocaust: A Christian Interpretation.* Minneapolis, Minn.: Fortress Press, 1994.

Hallie, Philip P. *Lest Innocent Blood Be Shed: The Story of the Village of Le Chambon and How Goodness Happened There.* New York: Harper & Row, 1979.

Hellman, Peter. *Avenue of the Righteous.* New York: Atheneum Books, 1980.

Herzer, Ivo, Klaus Voigt, and James Burgwyn, eds. *The Italian Refuge: Rescue of Jews During the Holocaust.* Washington, D.C.: The Catholic University of America Press, 1989.

Keneally, Thomas. *Schindler's List.* New York: Simon & Schuster, 1993.

Kurek, Ewa. *Your Life Is Worth Mine: How Polish Nuns in World War II Saved Hundreds of Jewish Lives in German-Occupied Poland, 1939-1945.* New York: Hippocrene, 1997.

Leboucher, Fernande. *Incredible Mission [of Father Benoit].* Trans. J. F. Bernard. Garden City, N.J.: Doubleday, 1969.

Lyman, Darryl. *Holocaust Rescuers: Ten Stories of Courage.* Springfield, N.J.: Enslow, 1999.

Marchione, Margherita. *Yours Is a Precious Witness: Memoirs of Jews and Catholics in Wartime Italy.* New York: Paulist, 1997.

Michalczyk, John J., ed. *Resisters, Rescuers, and Refugees: Historical and Ethical Issues.* Kansas City, Mo.: Sheed & Ward, 1997.

Oliner, Samuel P., and Pearl M. Oliner. *The Altruistic Personality: Rescuers of Jews in Nazi Europe.* New York: Free Press, 1992. Foreword by Harold M. Schulweis.

Paldiel, Mordecai. *The Path of the Righteous: Gentile Rescuers of Jews During the Holocaust.* Hoboken, N.J.: Ktav Publishing Co., 1993.

Phayer, Michael, and Eva Fleischner. *Cries in the Night: Women Who Challenged the Holocaust.* Kansas City, Mo.: Sheed & Ward, 1997.

Ramati, Alexander. *The Assisi Underground: The Priests Who Rescued Jews.* New York: Stein & Day, 1978.

Rosenfeld, Harvey. *Raoul Wallenberg.* Rev. ed. New York: Holmes & Meier, 1995.

Schulweis, Harold M. "They Were Our Brothers' Keepers." *Moment* 11:5 (May 1996): 47-50.

Stein, André. *Quiet Heroes: True Stories of the Rescue of Jews by Christians in Nazi-Occupied Holland.* New York: New York University Press, 1988.

Tec, Nechama. *When Light Pierced the Darkness: Christian Rescue of Jews in Nazi-Occupied Poland.* New York: Oxford University Press, 1986.

Ten Boom, Corrie. *The Hiding Place.* London: Hodder & Straughton, 1972.

Wood, E. Thomas, and Stanislaw M. Jankowski. *Karski: One Man Tried to Stop the Holocaust.* New York: J. Wiley, 1994. Foreword by Elie Wiesel.

Zuccotti, Susan. *The Italians and the Holocaust: Persecution, Rescue, and Survival.* New York: Basic Books, 1987.

SELECTED FILMS (sources in parentheses listed below)

In addition to the following representative list, more film references can be found on many websites in the next section.

The Assisi Underground. 115 min. Color. MGM Home Entertainment, 1982. Videocassette. The clandestine activities of priests and nuns to save Jews during the Nazi occupation of Italy. (SSSS)

Au Revoir Les Enfants. 103 min. B/W. Orion Home Video, 1989. Videocassette. True story of a Catholic schoolboy and his Jewish friend who was sheltered by a Carmelite priest in France. (SSSS)

The Courage to Care. 30 min. Color. Anti-Defamation League, 1986. Videocassette. Six individuals who knowingly risked their lives to rescue Jews. (ADL)

The Diary of Anne Frank. 151 min. B/W. Twentieth-Century Fox, 1959. Videocassette. Anne Frank and her family attempt to escape Nazi persecution by hiding in an attic for two years. (SSSS)

Holocaust. 7½ hrs. Color. Republic Pictures Home Video, 1978. Videocassettes (3). NBC-TV miniseries of the lives of two families living in Nazi Germany during the Holocaust. (SSSS)

Night and Fog. 32 min. Color, B/W. Home Vision, 1955. Videocassette. Elie Wiesel's classic of survival in the death camps. (SSSS)

Weapons of the Spirit. 90 min. Color, B/W. First Run Features, 1989. Videocassette. The moving story of a small Protestant village in France, Le Chambon-sur-Lignon, which sheltered 5,000 Jews under Nazi occupation. Optional study guide package. (SSSS)

Sources

ADL   Anti-Defamation League, 823 United Nations Plaza, New York, NY 10017

SSSS   Social Studies School Service, 10200 Jefferson Boulevard, Room J, P.O. Box 802, Culver City, CA 90232-0802

WEBSITES

Valuable resources are available from *Facing History and Ourselves* (some geared more to high school) and the U.S. Holocaust Memorial Museum, especially their *Teaching About the Holocaust: A Resource Book for Educators*, which includes an annotated bibliography and videography. See their websites.

U.S. Holocaust Memorial Museum
http://www.ushmm.gov

Jewish-Christian Relations
http://www.jcrelations.net/index.htm
Includes numerous useful documents, essays, and annotated bibliographies.

Yad Vashem Holocaust Museum in Jerusalem
http://www.yadvashem.org

Cybrary of the Holocaust
http://www.remember.org
Images, stories, and more.

McGill-Toolen High School Theology Library
http://www.mcgill.pvt.k12.al.us/jerryd/cathmob.htm

Resources for the Study of Antisemitism and the Holocaust
http://www.mcgill.pvt.k12.al.us/jerryd/cm/antisem.htm

The Holocaust/Shoah Page
http://www.mtsu.edu/~baustin/holo.html
Glossary, chronology, and documents.

Vatican: The Holy See
http://www.vatican.va
Official Vatican website for Church documentation.

National Conference of Catholic Bishops
http://www.nccbuscc.org

American Jewish Committee
http://www.ajc.org

Anti-Defamation League
http://www.adl.org

Holocaust Teacher Resource Center
http://www.holocaust-trc.org

Institute for Christian and Jewish Studies
http://www.icjs.org

Stockholm International Forum on the Holocaust
http://www.holocaustforum.gov.se

World Council of Churches
http://www.wcc-coe.org

National Catholic Center for Holocaust Education
http://maura.setonhill.edu/~holocst/

Service International de Documentation Judéo-Chrétienne
http://www.sidic.org
In English and French.

Center for Christian-Jewish Learning at Boston College
http://www.bc.edu/cjlearning